ART ATTACK ™

Great Gifts

Art Attack Tips and Tricks first published 1998 by Hamlyn Children's Books,
an imprint of Egmont Children's Books Limited.

Art Attack Great Gifts and Art Attack Your Room first published in 1999 by Hamlyn Children's Books,
an imprint of Egmont Children's Books Limited.

This edition first published in 2000 by Mammoth, an imprint of Egmont Children's Books Limited,
a division of Egmont Holding Limited, 239 Kensington High Street, London W8 6SA.

Illustrations and design: ARKADIA
Text for Art Attack Tips and Tricks: Mike Janson

ISBN 0 7497 4463 4

Printed in Slovenia

Contents

When you see this clock symbol, it means that you will have to leave your Art Attack to dry, often overnight.

WARNING
Be very careful when using sharp objects, such as scissors.

If you find it hard to cut through cardboard, try dampening it a little.

A safe way to make a hole in cardboard is to push the point of a hard pencil through the card into some sticky tack.

Perfect Papier Mâché

Many of the projects in this book need papier mâché. There are two ways of making this, but they both need the same glue mixture. Pour some PVA glue into a bowl, then add half as much water. Stir them together to make a really strong mixture.

NEIL'S TIP
You can get PVA glue from any art supplies shop and most large stationery stores.

NEIL'S TIP
Make sure you protect your work surface with some old newspaper. If you work on a plastic bag you can simply peel off your project.

METHOD 1
This is ideal if you want to make a mould of something or if you want to cover something quite smoothly (e.g. Heavy-Weight Trainer, page 14).

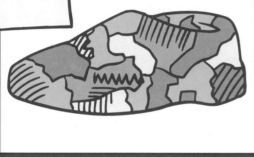

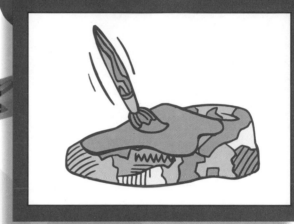

Coat the item in the glue mixture, and cover it in strips of newspaper or toilet roll. You will probably need two or three layers.

Then paint over everything again with the glue mixture, and leave it to dry.

METHOD 2
This is perfect for modelling 3D shapes (e.g. 3D Badges, page 8).

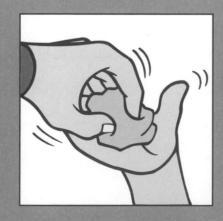

For this method, dip some newspaper or toilet roll into the glue mixture and squeeze out any excess glue. You can mould this into any shape you like and place it on your Art Attack. If you want, you can then cover everything in a layer of toilet roll to give a smoother outline, or just leave it to dry as it is.

Anything made with papier mâché will need time to dry out – at least overnight. So be patient.

Fantasy Flyer

Have you ever wondered how they design all those fantastic futuristic jets that you get in cartoons or computer games? They build a model first. Follow these steps to design a Fantasy Flyer for a fellow fanatic.

WHAT YOU NEED
wedge-shaped chocolate box, pencil, cardboard, ruler, scissors, plastic cup, toilet roll tubes, sweet tubes, pen tops, bottle top, egg box, sticky tape, glue, acrylic paint, old felt-tip pens

1

Lie the chocolate box on a piece of cardboard and draw a chunky pointed wing on each side. Take away the box and join up the wings.

2

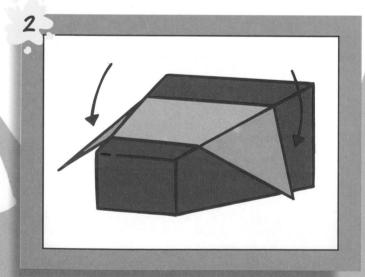

Cut the whole thing out and bend the wings slightly along the lines. Use a ruler to help you. Stick this on top of your chocolate box with the wings slanting down.

3

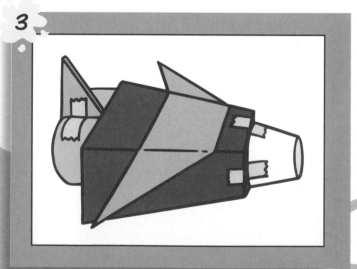

Tape a plastic cup to the front of the box for the nose. Cut a toilet roll tube in half and tape the sections to the back of the box for the jets. Cut out a triangle of cardboard and slot it between the tubes to make the tail. Stick it firmly in place.

4

To make your Fantasy Flyer look like a real aeroplane, stick on lots of tubes in all shapes and sizes. Some could go under the wings to look like jets and fuel tanks. Some could be cut in half to make interesting shapes.

5

And to make it look really futuristic, stick on lots of other bits and pieces, for example a bottle-top nose, an egg box cockpit.

6

Make sure everything is stuck down firmly, then paint it – any colour you like. Add details in felt-tip or marker pen.

NEIL'S TIP
Instead of using acrylic paint, you can mix poster paint with PVA glue.

NEIL'S TIP
You might need to give your plane a few layers of paint, or start by giving it a white undercoat – especially if all your boxes and tubes are different colours.

Screaming Bookmark

Some people are always losing their place when they read a book. What they need is a bookmark – a screaming one!

1 Cut a strip of card roughly 6cm wide and twice the height of your book. Fold it in half, top to bottom. Then mark a point roughly a third of the way down from the fold and fold the top piece up again.

2 Draw the top lip of a mouth above the fold, and a bottom lip below the fold. Then draw the top and bottom half of a head, and make it look as gruesome as possible.

3 Open out your bookmark and draw an explosion box in the mouth. Write in it what you want to say. Then join up the two halves of the head behind the box. Add the details (tongue, teeth, tonsils) and colour everything in.

4 Fold your bookmark back together and hook it over the page of your book. Then, when you pull your bookmark out from the top, it screams at you.

> I know another way to make a bookmark scream – tell it a good ghost story! Ha ha ha!

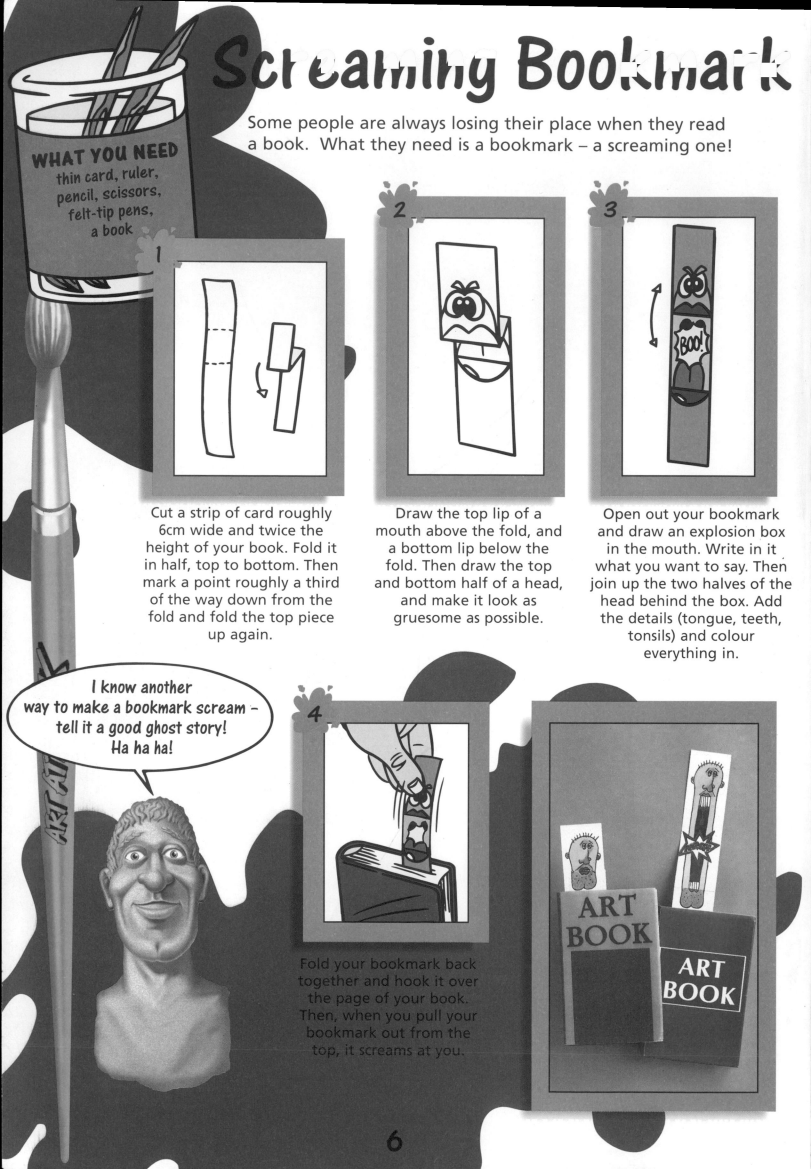

3D Books

If you want to give someone a really special present, without spending a fortune, try one of these 3D Books.

WHAT YOU NEED
blank book (hardback or paperback), papier mâché, pencil, paint, gold or silver pen, permanent marker

ALWAYS MAKE SURE YOU HAVE A WINDOW OPEN WHEN USING PERMANENT MARKERS!

1

Cover the front and back of your blank book in strips of papier mâché (see page 3) and leave to dry overnight.

2

Now draw your design on to your book. This one is going to be an ancient diary with fancy hinges, corner pieces and a lock.

3

When your design is finished, build it up by taking bits of tissue or newspaper and dipping them into the glue mixture. Squeeze out the excess, then press into shape on the cover. Leave to dry overnight again.

4

When the book is dry, you can paint it.

5

Add the metal details in gold or silver pen. Use a permanent marker to add outline or shadows.

Brilliant 3D Badges

Badges are great and they make really fun presents, especially these fantastic 3D Art Attack badges!

1

WHAT YOU NEED
cardboard, pencil, scissors, large safety pin, sticky tape, PVA glue, toilet paper, papier mâché, paint, black marker pen, plastic bag to work on

Draw your badge shape on to a piece of cardboard. Cut it out and tape a safety pin to the back, as near the middle as possible.

2

3

Brush some PVA glue over the back of your badge. Place a piece of toilet paper on top, butting up to the pin. Then place another piece on the other side of the pin. Leave to dry, then trim off the edges.

Now for the front of your badge! Mould a 3D shape out of papier mâché, then leave it to dry and harden overnight.

4

NEIL'S TIP

Make sure you stick down the fixed side of the pin, not the side that opens. Otherwise, you won't be able to wear your badge!

When it's completely dry, paint on your design and draw round the edge with a black marker pen.

Try any design you like!

Giant Pencil

Do you know someone who never has a pen or pencil? Well, give them one of these giant Art Attack pencils and they'll never be stuck for something to write with.

1

2

WHAT YOU NEED
front and back of a cereal box, pencil, ruler, sticky tape, scissors, felt-tip pen, newspaper, papier mâché, paint, gold or silver pen

Divide one of the cereal box sides widthways into six equal strips. Fold the card along these lines. Overlap and tape the two end strips. This is the body of the pencil.

Cut out a quarter of the other piece of cereal box and roll it into a cone. Place it in one end of the pencil and let it spring out to fit snugly. Tape it in place.

3

4

5

Snip enough off the end to fit your felt-tip pen. Slip the pen inside (with the lid on) and tape that in place too, with at least half a centimetre poking out above the lid.

Now stuff the pencil tightly with scrunched-up newspaper. When it is packed, tape across the top to keep everything in. Cover all except the tip in papier mâché and leave to dry overnight.

When it's dry you can paint it and add lettering in gold or silver – just like a real pencil.

It even writes, and if it ever runs out, just pull out the pen and replace it with another.

Wind-Up Tongue Card

This is the perfect way to wind up your family and friends.

1

Fold a piece of card in half. Draw a line on the inside about 9cm long (that's a bit longer than your finger). This is the mouth. Draw or paint a funny face around it – the uglier the better!

2

Make a hole at each end of the line, 1cm below it. Make another hole in the middle of the line. Put your scissors through and snip along the line – but don't go quite as far as the other two holes.

WHAT YOU NEED
card, pencil, paint or felt-tip pens, sticky tack, scissors, elastic band, paper clips, sticky tape

3

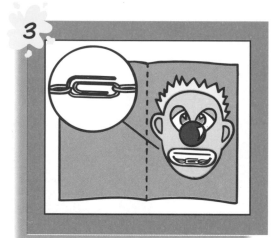

From the back of the card, poke the ends of an elastic band through the two holes and slip them on to the paper clip.

4

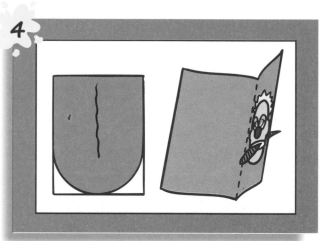

On another piece of card, draw a rectangle 8cm by 11cm with a tongue shape at the bottom. Cut it out and colour it in. Slot the tongue into the mouth and tape it at the back.

5

Now your card's ready. Twist the elastic band with the paper clip. When it's fully wound up, trap it with the tongue, close the card and keep it shut with another paper clip.

Now you just have to decide who you want to wind up today. Stand back and wait for the raspberry!

Gift Wrapping Paper

This Art Attack could save you a lot of pocket money. Try making your own wrapping paper.

WHAT YOU NEED
a large sheet of paper, felt-tip pens, gold or silver pen

1

With a felt-tip pen, draw a cross down the middle of your sheet of paper. I like red felt tip on white paper.

2

In the two top sections, draw loops that join in the middle. In the two bottom sections, draw long thin triangles that also join in the middle. Then colour the whole thing in.

3

Decorate all the red that you've drawn with your gold or silver pen. Then carefully draw a circle in the middle. This is your bow.

4

Add shadows to your bow to make it stand out from the paper. Do this by drawing a dark line on all the bottom and left-hand edges.

Now draw and decorate a rectangle in the bottom right-hand section of the paper and write your message inside. Draw a little circle and some string to the middle, and there you have some DIY wrapping paper, complete with its own gift tag.

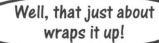

Well, that just about wraps it up!

Stained-Glass Picture

Why not liven up someone's view with this Stained-Glass Picture?

WHAT YOU NEED
paper, pencil, tissue paper, PVA glue, sticky-backed plastic, cardboard, scissors

1

Draw a simple design for your picture. Then tear pieces of tissue paper roughly into the shapes that you have drawn.

2

Pour a cup of PVA glue on to a sheet of sticky-backed plastic (shiny side up). Paste it into a rectangle the same size as your design. Stick the tissue paper shapes down. Fill in the gaps with small scraps of tissue paper for a mosaic effect.

3

Carefully pour more PVA glue on top and spread it out without moving the shapes. Leave it to dry – for about 3 days!

4

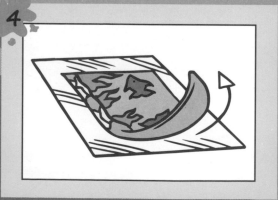

Now just hold your picture up to the light to get a great stained-glass effect.

When your picture is dry, peel it away from the sticky-backed plastic and turn it over, so that the underneath side is facing upwards. Cut out a cardboard frame and stick it on.

Slot Plants

Are you ever stuck for an idea for a present? Well, everyone loves a plant, and you don't even have to water these!

WHAT YOU NEED
cardboard box, scissors, pencil, ruler, paint, marker pen

1 Cut two sides off a cardboard box and draw a vertical line down the middle of each one.

2 Now draw a flower or plant using this line as centre. Do a simple, big, bold shape, and make sure that the bottom is absolutely straight. Cut out your shape and draw around it on the second piece of card, making sure that the two centre lines line up. Cut this out, too.

NEIL'S TIP
To make sure that the slot is the right thickness, stand a straight piece of card up on its edge along the line, and draw round it.

3 Using the centre lines, measure halfway up both cut-outs and mark a point. Draw from this point up to the top of one shape and down to the bottom of the other shape. Now cut a slot the exact thickness of the cardboard along the lines you have drawn.

4 Paint both sides of your plant. Don't forget the pot.

Blooming marvellous!

When they're dry, add details in permanent marker. Then just slot the two pieces together and stand them up.

Heavy-Weight Trainer

Next time you are about to throw out an old pair of worn trainers or shoes – don't! Turn them into fantastic heavy-weight doorstops, bookends or paperweights.

WHAT YOU NEED
an old shoe, small stones, paper cup, scissors, sticky tape, papier mâché, felt-tip pen, paint

1

Take an old shoe. Remove the laces, and fasten any buckles or straps. Pack the shoe with stones, right into all the nooks and crannies.

2

Place a paper cup inside the shoe, where your heel would normally go. You may have to take out a few stones. Cut or tear the cup so that it's level with the mouth of the shoe. Tape it firmly in place.

3

Cover the whole thing, even inside the cup, with two layers of papier mâché. Then leave it to dry overnight.

Draw on your design and paint your shoe in bright, bold colours.

NEIL'S TIP
If your shoe is a bit smelly, wash it first and let it dry.

Here's a footnote: These are definitely not running shoes!

Creepy Mobiles

If you want to give someone a terrifying scrap attack, these creepy mobiles are just perfect!

WHAT YOU NEED
scrap paper –
black, white and red, PVA glue,
felt-tip pen, cotton thread,
sticky tape

1

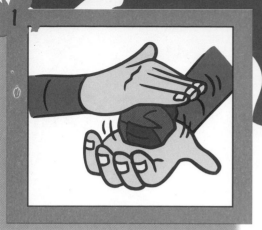

Scrunch up a piece of black scrap paper into a ball in the palm of your hand – this is the creature's 'body'.

2

Take a piece of black paper about 10cm square and twist to make it long and thin. Do the same with another five pieces of paper – these are the creature's 'legs'.

3

Dip one of the 'legs' in the PVA glue and stick it into a crack in the 'body'. Bend it down a little. Do the same for the other five 'legs', sticking three on each side of the 'body'.

4

Scrunch up two small pieces of white paper into very tight balls – these are the 'eyes'. With a felt-tip pen, draw on the 'eyeballs'. Cut a small piece of red paper into a rough oval shape – this is the 'tongue'. Dip the 'eyes' and 'tongue' in the PVA glue and stick them in place on the 'body'.

5

Brush PVA glue all over the creature, including the 'eyes' and 'tongue' and leave to dry overnight until it is hard and shiny.

Stick a length of cotton thread on to the creature's back with sticky tape, hang it up and wait for the screams!

To make other mobiles, you could add glitter eyes and scrap paper teeth, or tracing paper wings and a long curly tongue made by twisting a piece of paper round a pencil. Or make up your own creepy creatures!

15

Thumbs-Up Award

Say 'well done' to someone who has passed a test or achieved something really great with a Thumbs-Up Award.

WHAT YOU NEED
cardboard, pencil, scissors, newspaper, sticky tape, polystyrene cup, pebble, papier mâché, paint

Draw round your hand on to a piece of card. Include about 5cm of your wrist. Make sure your fingers are together and the thumb is sticking out to one side. Cut it out, snipping between the fingers.

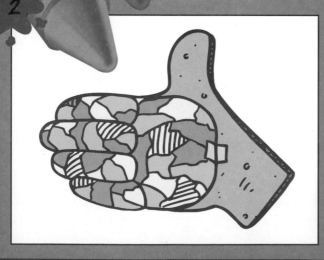

Scrunch up a sheet of newspaper and tape it to one side of the hand. Twist smaller bits of newspaper and tape them to each finger. This is now the back of your hand. Tape more newspaper twists to the fingers on the other side.

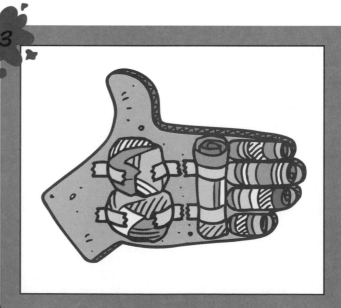

Scrunch half a page of newspaper into a sausage and tape it below the fingers. Tape two small balls of newspaper just above the wrist in the same place as the bumps on your own hand. Wrap more sticky tape round the fingers and palm to make it sturdier.

4

Now bend the fingers (not the thumb) one by one, and hold them closed. Tape them into position.

5

Tape the polystyrene cup upside down in the middle of a square of cardboard. Tear off the top, then cut about a quarter of the way down each side. Put a pebble in the cup to act as a weight and stuff a ball of newpaper on top of it to keep it in place.

6

Push the wrist of the hand into the slot in the cup, and tape it firmly in place.

7

Cover the whole thing, including the base, in two layers of papier mâché, moulding some more knuckles and bumps if you want. Leave it to dry.

When dry, paint the base black and the hand gold or silver. You can add some shading in the nooks and crannies, too.

NEIL'S TIP

Make your own gold-effect paint by adding a tiny bit of black and green to your yellow paint.

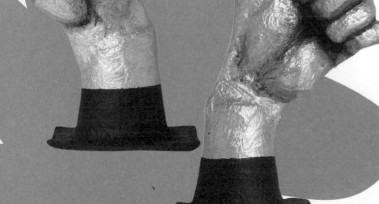

WAX CRAYON

17

A Celebration Breakfast

Why not make a celebration breakfast for someone special?
An Art Attack Celebration Breakfast, that is.

WHAT YOU NEED
white card, pencil, cotton wool, tissue paper (various colours), PVA glue, felt-tip pens, scissors, backing paper or board

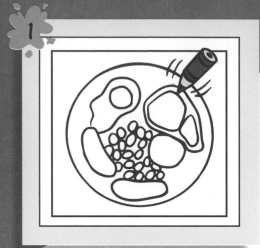

1 Draw a dinner plate sized circle on your white card. On this plate roughly draw an egg, sausages, beans, a chop and a tomato.

2 Dab some PVA glue mixed with a touch of water on to just one area of the picture. Stick on some cotton wool.

3 Cover the cotton wool with coloured tissue paper and paste down the edges, stuffing the cotton wool in as you go.

4 Build up the whole picture in this way, section by section.

5 When the glue is dry, add some more detail with a felt-tip pen, or scraps of tissue paper.

Mmmm! Looks nice enough to eat!

When you've finished, cut the whole thing out. If you like, you can stick it on to some coloured paper or board.

Dream Island

Do you know anyone who loves going on holiday?
Now you can make them their own paradise island in the sun.

1

Start by drawing a rough outline of your island on the cardboard. Leave enough space around the edge for the sea.

2

You then create the shape of your island using scrunched-up balls of newspaper. Dip the bottom of each ball into some PVA glue mixed with water. Then stick it in place.

3

When you are happy with the overall shape of your island, cover it all in strips of papier mâché. Push it into the newspaper to make coves and interesting rock formations. Leave to dry overnight.

4

Add some trees, made from small balls of newspaper covered in PVA mixture. Also add some buildings – small square scraps of card and a folded piece of card for the roofs. Leave to dry again.

5

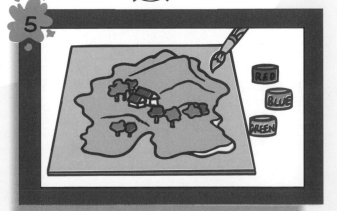

Now paint your island. To create shimmering surf, stick bits of clingfilm on to the sea and wrinkle it up to form waves.

6

And here's a very special paradise island.

Heart-Throb Brooch

Do you know anyone with a secret heart-throb?
Try making this Heart-Throb Brooch for them.

WHAT YOU NEED
an empty matchbox, paper, pencil, scissors, safety pin, sticky tape, glue, card, glitter, picture

NEIL'S TIP
If you do this on coloured paper or wrapping paper, you won't need to paint it later.

1

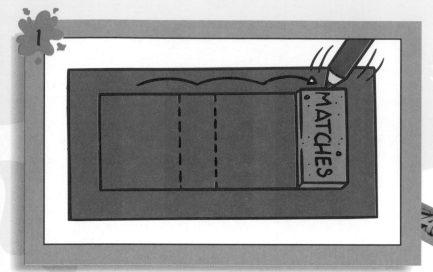

Place the matchbox on your paper and draw around three sides. Roll the matchbox along the paper, drawing along the edges as you go. Cut out this long strip of paper, and it should fit perfectly round the matchbox.

2

3

Now make the shape for the front of your brooch. Cut it out, cover it with glue and dip it in some glitter. When it's dry, stick it to the front of the box.

Tape a safety pin to the back of the box. Make sure you tape the side of the pin that doesn't open. Cover one side of the paper in glue and wrap it round the box, starting at the pin.

4

Stick your heart-throb picture on the inside of the matchbox. Then you can slip the inside back into the box and no one will know that the picture is there.

I liked mine so much I kept it myself.

20

WHAT YOU NEED
A3 paper, felt-tip pens, pencil, scissors, glue, photos

Comic Strip Photo Frames

Do you want to see someone star in a comic strip? Well, here's your chance.

Fold your piece of paper in half lengthways. Then fold it in half the other way. Fold the top flap down in half, then turn over the paper and do the same to the other flap.

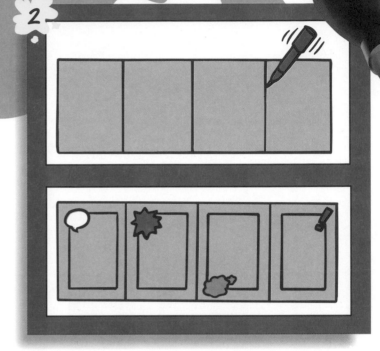

Lay your strip flat with the folded side to the bottom. Draw a felt-tip line along the top of the paper, as close to the edge as possible. Draw lines down each crease, too. Draw a pencil frame about 2cm wide in each of the boxes and add some comic strip special effects, such as speech and thought bubbles, or explosion boxes. Go over these neatly in felt-tip.

NEIL'S TIP
Don't worry if the lines are wobbly. It all adds to the effect.

Open out the paper. To cut out the windows, make a hole the safe way (see page 2) and use this as a starting point for your scissors. Dab some glue carefully down each crease and down the side edges. Leave the top open. Fold the paper back over and press it down. Leave it overnight with some books on top.

When the glue is dry, trim some photos to fit the frames and slide them in. Write some messages in the special effects boxes and you've got your own personal comic strip.

Surprise Birthday Cards

These pictures look quite normal, but open the flap and you get a big surprise. These surprise pictures make ideal birthday cards for your friends.

1

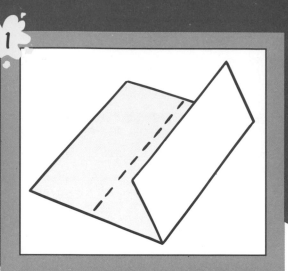

WHAT YOU NEED

thin card, ruler, pencil, felt-tip pens

Take a piece of thin card (any size you like) and divide it into thirds along the top. Fold over the right-hand third.

2

Think of an idea for your card and draw it across the front on both pieces. Make sure that anything that you want to change on the inside goes on the right hand flap.

Snappy birthday!

3

fold

fold

Open out the flap so that you only have half a picture. Now you can change whatever you like on the right-hand side of the picture. First draw in all the bits that you don't want to change. Then draw in your surprise and colour it in.

ART ATTACK

22

Design a T-Shirt

No ideas for your best friend's birthday present? Why not create a fantastic exclusive T-shirt with this simple method?

NEIL'S TIP

If you draw your design on to your T-shirt in pencil, you can rub it out if you make a mistake.

WHAT YOU NEED

a plain T-shirt, cardboard, pencil, permanent markers, gold pen

Put a piece of cardboard inside a plain white T-shirt. This helps to stretch the area you want to draw on. It also stops the ink going through to the back of your T-shirt.

Now draw your design on to the T-shirt using lightly flicked lines.

Take care when washing your new fancy T-shirt. Make sure the water isn't too hot. You may find that the colour fades over time, but then you can just go over the design with your pens again.

When you've finished your outline, fill it in with coloured permanent marker. Add special jazzy gold pen for a bit of extra dazzle.

Art Chart

Name	Great Gift
....	....
....	....
....	....
....	....
....	....
....	....
....	....
....	....
....	....
....	....
....	....
....	....
....	....
....	....
....	....

Tips and Tricks

Hi! Welcome to Art Attack! In this book I'll let you in on some of my favourite secrets for getting the most out of your drawings. Come with me, and pick up some top Art Attack tips and tricks.

Neil Buchanan

Sausage and Egg Pictures

I often think about sausages and eggs. And that's not because I'm hungry. It's just that simple egg shapes and simple sausage shapes help me with my drawing. I'll show you how.

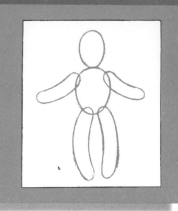

If I want to draw a person, I find the best thing to do is to draw it in rough, using sausage and egg shapes. The head is an egg, the body a bigger egg and the arms and legs sausages.

Draw the sausages and eggs lightly in pencil so they are easy to rub out.

When I'm happy with the rough shape, I use it as a guide to add on clothes and other details.

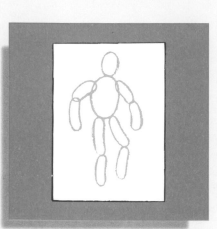

This idea is great for drawing people in awkward positions, like this footballer.

Now I can add the clothes and rub out the pencil lines.

It's a great way to help you draw things in rough first.
And it doesn't just work for people. Look at these.

Here's a horse. See how you can use eggs for the head, neck and body and sausages for the tail and legs.

It even works for trees. A long sausage for the trunk and branches and eggs for the leaves.

And finally...
a sausage and egg sports car!

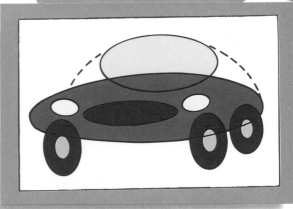

NOW TRY IT YOURSELF.

ELEPHANT

BALLET DANCER

Breakfast will never be the same again. But then, I eat porridge!

3

Curvy Pictures

Do some of your ideas fall flat? Do you ever draw a picture of something that's meant to be rounded, but it never is? Well, here's a simple way to round out your pictures.

Here's my picture of a tomato. Looks flat, eh? But watch this.

What we need is a few curves. See how the curved lines across the tomato make it begin to look rounded.

I've just begun to make this tree look rounded. Why don't you finish it off for me?

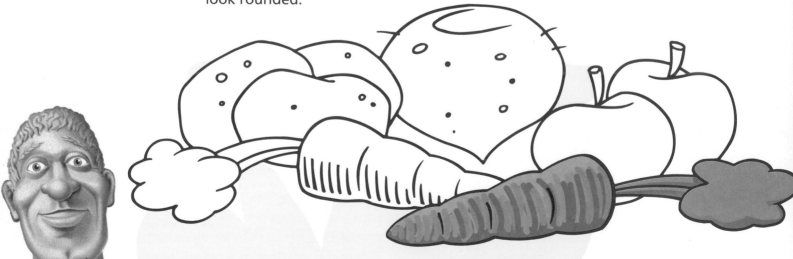

So it's easy to stop things being flat. I hope it works on my lemonade!

Look what I've done to this carrot. Instead of using lines I've used curved colouring.

TRY IT ON THE REST OF THE VEGETABLES AND FRUIT.

Cross-Hatching

A great thing about an ordinary crayon or pencil is that you can get different shades and textures just by pressing lighter or harder. But what can you do if you only have a felt-tip or a ball-point pen? You can't press harder or lighter because the ink comes out the same way! So try this.

1

Just draw lines across the area you want to shade darker. See, it looks darker already.

2

Now draw lines across the first lines you drew … in the opposite direction. Does it look even darker?

3

If I add more lines in another direction it gets darker still.

Practise cross-hatching with a ball-point pen. You can draw really quickly with it.

I've shaded in this policeman. See how some areas look darker.

TRY IT YOURSELF.

Cartoon Eyes

There are lots of different ways to draw eyes. Try drawing a lemon shape with a wheel inside. The outside bit of the wheel is the coloured bit – the iris – and the inside is black – the pupil. And don't forget the eyelid, eyelashes and the eyebrows! If you are cartooning, there are lots more ways to draw eyes.

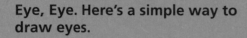

Eye, Eye. Here's a simple way to draw eyes.

First it's a sort of M-shape with a line underneath. Next draw a line across the M.

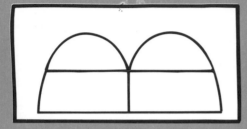

Then draw a circle for the pupil. Forget the iris – the coloured bit – and just put a thin V inside the circle. Doesn't that look sparkly?

NOW TRY SOMETHING EVEN SIMPLER.
Draw two circles in each box.

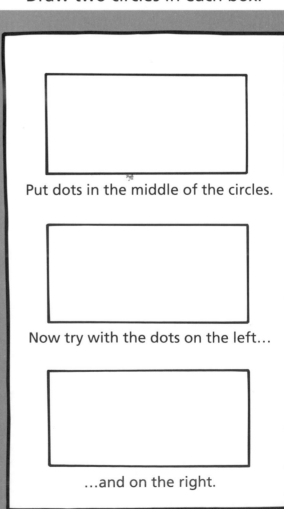

Put dots in the middle of the circles.

Now try with the dots on the left…

…and on the right.

Leave a little bit of white when you fill in the black of the pupil so that it looks like it's gleaming.

TELL-TALE EYES

You can tell a lot from someone's eyes. Do you think I can tell a story by just drawing eyes? Let's try it. You draw in the other eye each time.

1. It's early morning. The alarm rings loudly to wake Tom with a start.

Eyes wide, pupils small, eyebrows up.

2. Arthur is lazy and is still fast asleep.

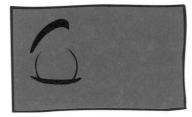

Eyelids heavy and closed.

3. Tom has a sneaky idea to wake up his brother Arthur.

Eyebrows down, eyes narrow, until they are almost slits.

4. Tom bangs on Arthur's bedpost. Clang!

Eyebrows up, eyes wobbly, pupils look like they're spinning.

5. Arthur is very angry.

Eyebrows down, nearly covering eyes.

6. Tom is worried.

Eyes sparkly, eyebrows up with a tear appearing.

7. Tom can't bear to look because Arthur is so angry.

Scrunched-up eyes, peeping out of one.

8. Well, Arthur's asleep again.

Eye think that's amazing!

NOW YOU TRY IT.
Make up your own story using only eyes!

7

Getting Lippy

When you're smiling, looking sad, kissing, whistling or sucking on a straw, your lips change shape. In fact, you can pull all kinds of faces by moving your lips. Now, here's my tip for drawing lips in any shape.

Draw top lips thinner than bottom lips.

WAX CRAYON

You could draw a mouth like this. But it doesn't look very real, does it?

What you need is lips. Add two teardrops facing each other. Use these as a guide to draw your lips, like this.

When you smile, the teardrops stretch outwards and slightly upwards.

When you are sad or frown, they stretch down.

When your mouth is open, the teardrops split and are stretched up and down.

When kissing, the teardrops are pressed together and look like four flower petals.

NOW YOU TRY IT.

Make me laugh.

Make me sad.

Give me a kiss.

Old Masters

This is me now. But what will I look like when I'm old? Well, I'm going to find out, so it should be quite a laugh. And you can try it on yourself. Grow old overnight … or at least in the next few minutes.

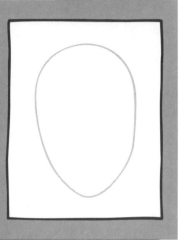

1

 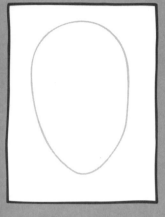

Draw a simple sketch of yourself like I have.

2

Rub out some of the hairline to make some bald bits. Colour the hair and eyebrows in silver crayon.

3

 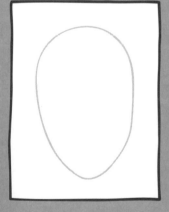

Draw in some frown lines and wrinkles and add some bags under the eyes.

4

 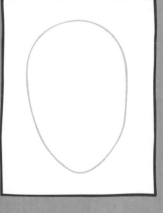

Add a silver beard and moustache.

5

 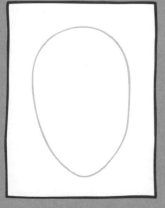

Do I look distinguished with reading glasses? Well, 40 years older!

The really weird thing is I look just like my dad. But he hasn't got a beard!

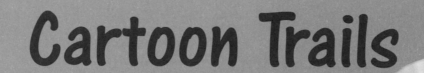

Cartoon Trails

It's easy to make your pictures show whether they are coming or going. Let's see how, by making trails.

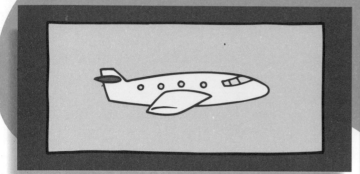

This aeroplane is just hanging in midair and doesn't appear to be going anywhere.

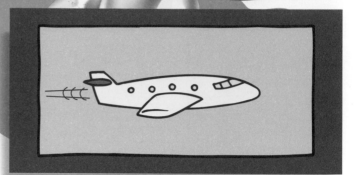

But if I add two light lines behind it, and a few lightly drawn letter Cs between them, you can see where it has come from.

Try it yourself on the first picture.

Look at the pendulum on this clock. The slightly curved direction lines show how it is swinging.

Let's make this person wave. Draw two direction lines either side of his hand. Add some little Cs to show where his hand was before. Now he's really waving.

Now try adding the movement to this cartoon.

Try using these to help bring the cartoon alive.

 Swing

 Rebound

Bounce

 Lazily

Collide

Chase

GARY THE GOLFER

Here's Gary the Golfer. He whacks the ball and his club swings round.

The ball zooms away, hits a tree and heads off in another direction.

The ball bounces down some steps and flies off.

A bee is lazily flying through some falling autumn leaves.

The ball whacks the bee, and carries on while the bee falls to the ground.

Now we've got an angry bee which chases Gary through the trees.

Make up your own cartoon in the frames below.

Fast and Flashy

Next time you're in a car or a train, travelling fast – but not too fast! – look out of the window. What do you see? Everything flashes past you and looks a bit blurred. So, to make your pictures move, I'm going to show you a few ideas.

Cut out a picture of something that can go fast, such as this speedboat. Put it on a plain piece of paper and pencil in a simple background. It looks still, doesn't it?

Now take away your cut-out and colour in the background, flashing it across the paper.

Make your colours and scribbles quite messy. Let bits of the paper show through:

Put your cut-out back on the paper. Is it moving now?

NOW YOU TRY IT WITH THESE PICTURES.

Just draw everything that would be in the background, for instance
cheering crowds and advertisements … but flash it across the paper.
You can use wax crayons, chalks, pencil crayons or even paint to
make flashy backgrounds.

13

Worn and Torn

Have you noticed how when you draw things, they look clean and new? In real life most objects have had a few knocks and bumps. So let me show you how to make things look worn out.

Here's a brand new cardboard box. I'm going to make it look old and tatty in 6 simple steps.

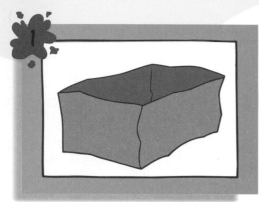

1 First, break up the straight lines with squiggles and make the box look slightly bent.

2 Now, tear the edges.

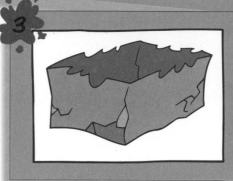

3 Add some cracks.

4 Put some knocks and bumps in with cross-hatching.

5 Add some patches.

6 Make it smelly by adding some flies and an old fishbone.

TRY IT YOURSELF.

Now, doesn't that look worn out?

WAX CRAYON

14

It's much more fun to do it to a person. And I think
The Head is perfect for this. But you can try it on your
teacher or your mum and dad!

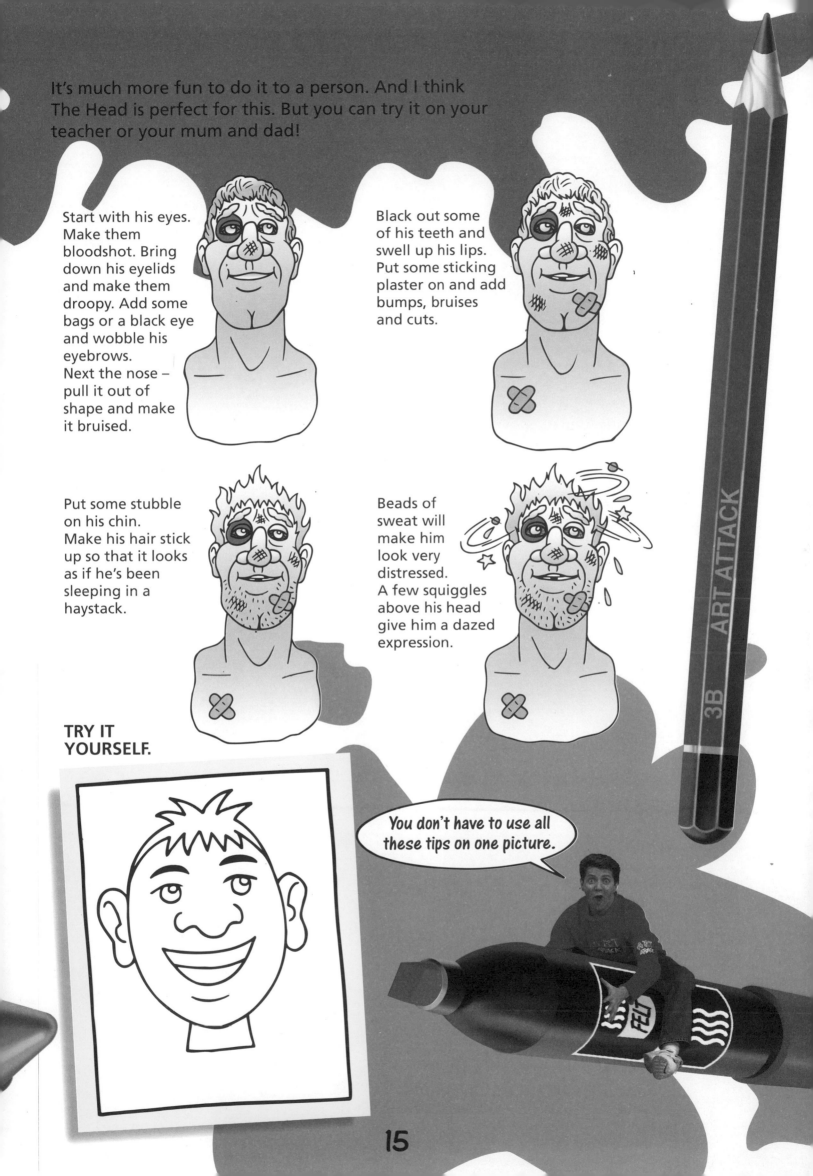

Start with his eyes.
Make them
bloodshot. Bring
down his eyelids
and make them
droopy. Add some
bags or a black eye
and wobble his
eyebrows.
Next the nose –
pull it out of
shape and make
it bruised.

Black out some
of his teeth and
swell up his lips.
Put some sticking
plaster on and add
bumps, bruises
and cuts.

Put some stubble
on his chin.
Make his hair stick
up so that it looks
as if he's been
sleeping in a
haystack.

Beads of
sweat will
make him
look very
distressed.
A few squiggles
above his head
give him a dazed
expression.

**TRY IT
YOURSELF.**

You don't have to use all
these tips on one picture.

Creased Up

What makes clothes actually look like clothes when we draw them? Well, look carefully at your clothes. They actually fit your body and have wrinkles and creases. Take a look at this.

Here is a shirt, but it looks as if it's been soaked in starch. It's just too stiff.

Here I've drawn it again. The lines aren't as straight and I've added some creases.

Now for some wrinkles, under the arms and on the arm joints.

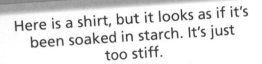

Here's a collection of different clothing.

Add creases to the backs of knees and under the legs and bottom area.

NOW CREASE UP THESE CHARACTERS.

Lucky I don't need clothes. I've got enough wrinkles on my face to worry about.

Moonlight Magic

Look out of your bedroom window at night. Can you see how objects are silhouetted against the sky? It's amazing how you can create a moody moonlit picture without using any colours.

1

Take a piece of dark-coloured paper – dark grey or blue. Draw a big fat moon in chalk. Add some fluffy clouds if you like and pick out some moonlight on their edges.

2

Now draw some outlines of trees in charcoal, pastels or black chalk. You can make them as simple or as complicated as you like.

3

Make the edge away from the moon darker – it's in shadow – and then draw some long shadows of the trees on the floor. Now, to finish, pick out some highlights down the edge of the trees facing the moonlight.

NOW YOU TRY IT.

Now that's moody.

WAX CRAYON

17

Shadows

What follows you around all day?
Well, it's missing from this picture.

Got it? Your shadow!

The first thing to do is to look where the light is coming from and where it can't get to. In the picture above, the light comes from the lamp on the right, so draw shadows on the man's left hand side under his hat and on his legs. And don't forget he'll cast a shadow on the pavement and up the wall, again on the side that the light can't get to.

Now go back and fill in the first picture with shadows.

AND HERE ARE SOME MORE FOR YOU TO TRY.

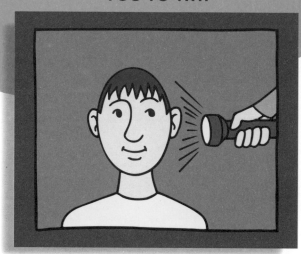

18

COWBOY SUNSET

In a lot of your pictures, the light will be coming from the sun. So you have to decide where the sun is in your pictures.

I've put the sun in this picture just peeping over the horizon, so the shadows will be long. This cowboy is getting a nice sun tan up front, but his back and bottom are in shade – as are the horses' rears.
Now, I've left one thing out, so you can fill in the shadow for the cactus to complete the picture.

19

Reflections

I like simple things that give a quick result and are very effective. So here's one that you can try, too. It's just amazing what a quick squiggle can do to a picture.

This picture might look like only half a girl; but hang on ...

... add a quick squiggle and there's a reflection in the water.

There are lots of things to do.

Here's a man running home in the rain ...

... so a squiggle underneath makes his reflection in the wet pavement.

Here's the sun and a boat in the sea.

And it works with reflections in mirrors, too.

TRY IT YOURSELF!

Bird's-eye View

When you look up at something, it looks different from when you look down on it. When you look down on something, it looks wider at the top than the bottom. So how do you draw it? Here's how. It's all in the triangle.

Keep the picture inside the triangle.

Draw a person inside this upside-down triangle. It might be strange to begin with.
Put the arms in first, then squeeze in the body, the head and the legs.
The person looks wider at the top.
See, you are looking down on the person.

Here are three upside-down triangles. See how I've drawn a building in the first one. It's a block of flats.

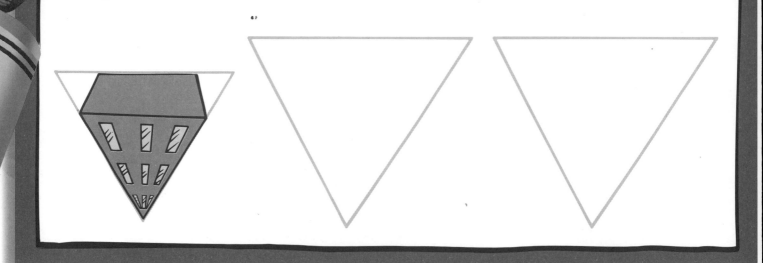

Try drawing more buildings in the other two triangles. Remember, you're looking down on them. Put in the windows. Follow the lines of the triangles.

Worm's-eye View

Now let's see how it works in reverse.

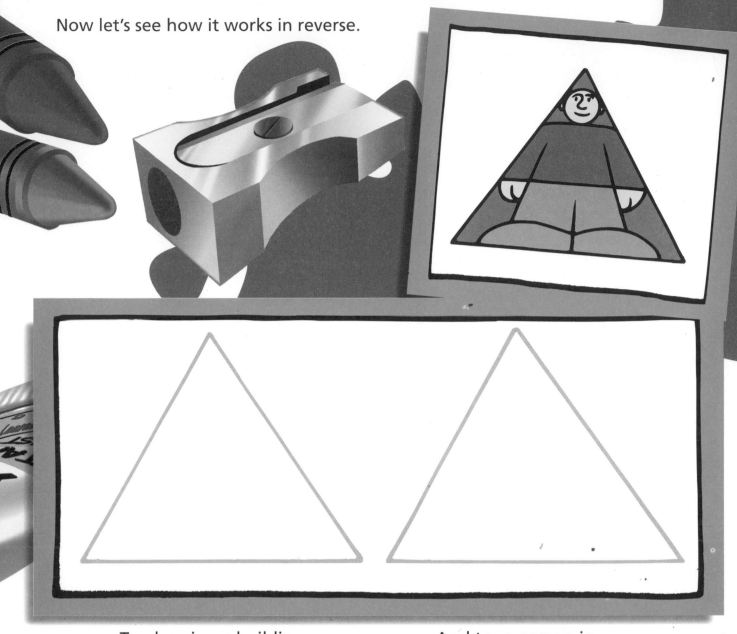

Try drawing a building
again in this triangle.

And try a person in
this one.

See what you're doing? You're looking up at them!

Good tip, Neil.
So an upside-down triangle means
you can look down on something and a
right way up triangle means you can look
up at something. So, with a right angle
triangle you must be able to see
round corners! Ha Ha Ha.

Spooky Art

Whooooo! So how do you get that Hallowe'en feeling? Well, I simply make things drip. All kinds of things – letters, trees, people – in fact anything c... c... can look g... g... ghostly!

Let's start with some spooky lettering. Any letter will do. Just make it drip off at the edges and go droopy. That's spooky.

Add drips of goo in different colours. I think green and yellow look scary.

TRY IT YOURSELF WITH SOME SPOOKY WORDS.
Choose your own colours, but red always looks like blood.

Keep adding the goo!

Now I can make a person look spooky, especially if I drip the eyes and mouth ...

... or a candle ...

... or a ghost look ghostly!

24

ART ATTACK 3B

CRAYON WAX CRAYON

ART ATTACK ™

Your Room

Hi! Welcome to
Art Attack! In this book I'll
show you some brilliant ideas
for your room. So come with
me, and create your own
very special space.

Neil Buchanan

CONTENTS

When you see this clock symbol, it means that you will have to leave your Art Attack to dry, often overnight.

WARNING
Be very careful when using sharp objects, such as scissors.

If you find it hard to cut through cardboard, try dampening it a little.

A safe way to make a hole in cardboard is to push the point of a hard pencil through the card into some sticky tack.

ART ATTACK

Perfect Papier Mâché

Many of the projects in this book need papier mâché.
There are two ways of making this, but they both need the same glue mixture.
Pour some PVA glue into a bowl, then add half as much water. Stir them together to make a really strong mixture.

NEIL'S TIP
You can get PVA glue from any art supplies shop and most large stationery stores.

METHOD 1
This is ideal if you want to make a mould of something or if you want to cover something quite smoothly (e.g. Bedside Lamp Tidy, page 10).

Make sure you protect your work surface with some old newspaper or a plastic bag.

Coat the item in the glue mixture, and cover it in strips of newspaper or toilet roll. You will probably need two or three layers.

Then paint over everything again with the glue mixture, and leave it to dry.

METHOD 2
This is perfect for modelling 3D shapes (e.g. Horror Hanger, page 20).

For this method, dip some newspaper or toilet roll into the glue mixture and squeeze out any excess glue. You can mould this into any shape you like and place it on your Art Attack.

If you want, you can then cover everything in a layer of toilet roll to give a smoother outline, or just leave it to dry as it is.

Anything made with papier mâché will need time to dry out – at least overnight. So be patient!

3

Big Mouth Noticeboard

Is your noticeboard all cluttered up? Do your pins keep falling out? What you need is a special Art Attack Big Mouth Noticeboard.

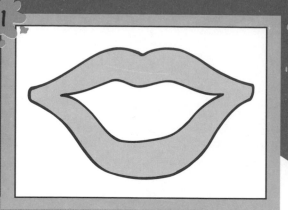

1

Cut out two sides of a large cardboard box. On one of the pieces, draw a huge mouth with big juicy lips. Cut this out. Then carefully cut out the inside of the mouth. This will be your 'lip' board.

2

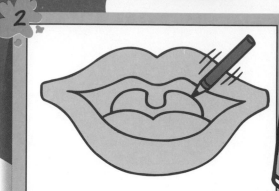

Draw around the lip board on to the other piece of cardboard and cut it out. This will be your 'mouth' board. On this, draw the inside of the mouth – but NOT the teeth!

WHAT YOU NEED
cardboard box, scissors, pencil, felt-tip pen, paint, glue

NEIL'S TIP

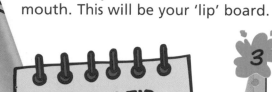

Before you paint your lips red, paint in two very rough white rectangles on the bottom lip. These highlights make the lips look really juicy.

3

Paint your mouth board with poster paint – black for the inside of the mouth and pink for the tongue. Paint your lip board bright red. Add the cracks on the lips with felt-tip pens or darker paint.

4

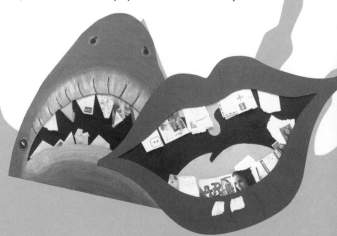

Paint a 2cm strip of glue round the edge of your mouth board. Press the lip board firmly on top and leave to dry overnight.

When it's dry, slot your photos, letters or notices under the lips. And there you have a Big Mouth Noticeboard, complete with paper teeth, and not a pin in sight.

Excellent Noticeboards! The mouth looks rather familiar...

Make Your Own Stencil

Have you ever used a stencil to decorate anything? You just hold it in place and dab paint through the hole, and the stencil creates a picture for you. Well, you can buy stencils in shops, but it's much more fun to make your own – and very simple, too.

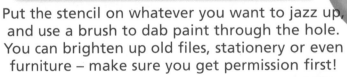

1

Cut out a picture from a magazine – anything that takes your fancy, but it's best if it's not too complicated.

NEIL'S TIP
Cut from the edge of the card into the middle of your shape. When you've finished cutting out your shape, tape the cut edges back together.

2

Draw around your picture on to a piece of card and cut out the inside shape.

3

Put the stencil on whatever you want to jazz up, and use a brush to dab paint through the hole. You can brighten up old files, stationery or even furniture – make sure you get permission first!

4

Now you have a brilliant home-made stencil that's just as effective as the ones you can buy in the shops.

Looks like a 'hole' lot of fun!

Paint Tube

Are your pencils and art materials lying all over the place? What you need is a paint tube to keep them in – a special Art Attack Paint Tube!

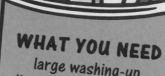

WHAT YOU NEED
large washing-up liquid bottle, scissors, sticky tape, newspaper, ruler, drink bottle lid, papier mâché, cereal box, paint

1

Take the top off the washing-up liquid bottle and wash it out thoroughly. When it's dry, carefully cut off the bottom of the tube. Then carefully cut round the top so that you've got the neck and a couple of centimetres down the side. Don't cut all the way round – leave a 'hinge' of about 2cm.

2

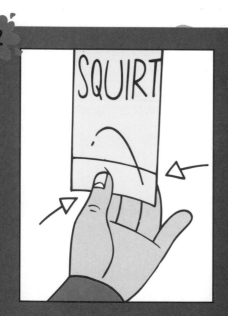

Squeeze the bottom together and tape it securely. Fold a small sheet of newspaper in half, place a ruler along the short edge and roll it up, then take the ruler out. Wrap the paper round the bottom of the tube and tape the edges together.

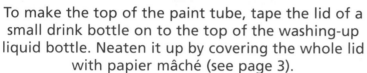

To make the top of the paint tube, tape the lid of a small drink bottle on to the top of the washing-up liquid bottle. Neaten it up by covering the whole lid with papier mâché (see page 3).

Cover the tube with papier mâché in the same way, going right over the top edge and a couple of centimetres down inside the tube.

 Leave to dry and harden overnight.

5

To make the lid close properly, you need a cardboard collar. Draw around a 30cm ruler on to some cereal box card and cut it out. Roll this into a coil, place it into the tube and let it spring out to measure the size of the collar. Cut off any overlap and tape the ends together. Stick the collar inside the tube, leaving about 2cm sticking out – about the same height as the side rim of the lid.

When it's dry, you can paint the whole thing in your own way, or copy a real paint tube to make it look realistic. Use it to store your pencils, felt-tip pens, paintbrushes and other art materials.

And I thought you just found paint in a paint tube!

Snooper-Proof Box

Do you need a special place to stash all your secrets away from snooping eyes and sticky fingers? Why not make your own Snooper-Proof Box?

WHAT YOU NEED
cardboard box, sticky tape, pencil, sticky tack, scissors, small boxes (e.g. matchboxes, toilet roll tubes), glue, tinsel, plastic bag, paint

1

Tape up the bottom of a cardboard box, but leave the top flaps open. Place a clenched fist on to the middle of one side of the box. Make four marks around your fist at the top, bottom and on each side.

NEIL'S TIP
Make sure the hole is no bigger than your circle. When it's cut out, it will be the perfect size for your hand, but too small for adult hands.

2

Join up the marks in a rough circle shape. Carefully pierce the cardboard with a sharp pencil and a ball of sticky tack then cut out this hole. If the cardboard's really tough, try wetting it a little.

3

Stick some smaller boxes on to the floor and inside walls of your box to hide your things in. Make sure you can reach them when you put your hand through the hole.

4

Cut some tinsel and a plastic bag into strips and stick these on to the inside of the front top flap. When you close the flaps, push that one down first, then the others on top of it and tape them securely.

Paint a design on the front. You could make the hole a monster's mouth. If any small-handed snoopers are brave enough to feel inside, they'll soon scream at the horrible-feeling strips guarding the entrance!

Rubbish Cupboard

Is your bedroom cluttered up with lots of pens, pencils and other bits and pieces? You need a Rubbish Cupboard.

WHAT YOU NEED
large cardboard box, scissors, smaller packaging boxes, pencil, paint, marker pen, PVA glue

1

Take a large cardboard box and pull out the top and bottom flaps. Cut out this whole piece. This will be your cupboard and the flaps will be the doors.

2

Trim the tops off an assortment of empty packaging boxes and place them where you want them on the bottom of your cupboard. This will form your bottom shelf.

3

Now place some boxes higher up to form your top shelf. Draw in the position of the shelf.

4

The inside will be dark, so paint it brown or black. Paint the outside any colour you like and add details in marker pen – like silver for the hinges.

Stick the boxes back in place. Brush a layer of PVA glue over everything to strengthen it and give a hard, shiny finish. When it's dry, you can fill the boxes with all your clutter.

Bedside Lamp Tidy

Is your bedside table a chaotic clutter? What you need is an Art Attack Bedside Lamp to hold your drink, your alarm clock and all your other bits and pieces.

WHAT YOU NEED

4 polystyrene cups, scissors, pencil, kitchen roll tube, sticky tape, cereal box card, small square-based biscuit box, papier mâché, paint, marker pen

Cut the top quarter off two polystyrene cups. Then make a hole with your thumb in the bottom of each cup. Push an old pencil through one of the cups, near the bottom.

Scrunch up a kitchen roll tube. Push the ends through the two cups and tape them. Tape everything on to a base made with cereal box card.

For the lampshade, cut another cup in half. In the bottom half, cut three snips an equal distance apart and tape it on top of the lamp post.

Tape the other half of that cup upside down on the card and stand another cup inside it. That's a rubbish bin to hold all your bits and pieces.

For the bin to hold your drink, cut out a strip of card big enough to wrap around your favourite cup. Wrap the card loosely round the cup. Tape the card, then tape it to your base.

6

Cut the bottom off the biscuit box – about 6cm.
Then snip about 1cm down the edges. Fold back
three of the sides and tape it in position on its side.

7

Stick two little balls of scrunched-up tape on
to the lamp bars (pencil). Stick two rolled-up
sausages of tape on to the bins as handles.

8

Cover the whole model in two layers of
papier mâché, including the base.
Leave it to dry overnight.

9

When dry, trim the base and paint
your model.

When the paint
is dry, you can add
some detail in
permanent marker,
especially on the
bins and the
pavement.

What a nifty way of keeping
your night-time knick-knacks
nice and neat!

Ruler Calendar

What's the best way of remembering dates?
Buy a calendar? Keep a diary? No, use a big ruler!

WHAT YOU NEED
large piece of cardboard, 30cm ruler, pencil, scissors, sticky tape, PVA glue, papier mâché, paint, marker pen, 2 large plastic paper clips

1

Measure and cut out a strip of cardboard four times the length and width of an ordinary ruler. Tape over any folds in the cardboard to strengthen it.

2

Now cut out another piece of cardboard, the same length but only half the width. Place this down the centre of the first piece and glue it in position.

3

Cover the whole ruler with papier mâché and leave to dry overnight. When it's dry, paint it any colour you like – wooden finish or plastic finish.

4

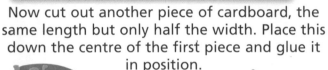

NEIL'S TIP
Remember that if your ruler is four times the normal size, each inch and each centimetre will be four times the normal size, too.

Now mark a point 1cm in from the edge. Then mark 12 inches down one side and 31 centimetres down the other. Don't forget to add extra markings such as millimetres and quarter inches. You could even draw a logo on it, or your name.

Remember to base it on a long ruler, otherwise you'll only have half a month and half a year.

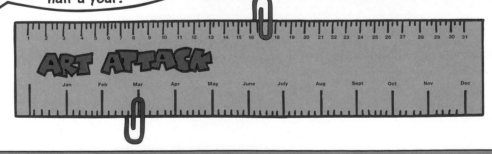

Slide your paper clips on to the ruler to show the day on the centimetre side and the month on the inch side. Then you can hang it on your wall and change it every day.

Plaster of Paris Picture

This is a great but simple idea for making a really effective plaque for your room.

WHAT YOU NEED

round margarine tub, plasticine, blunt pencil, plaster of Paris, string, paint, gold or silver pen

1 Roll a handful of plasticine into a ball. Press it out into a circle on a flat surface. When it is about 1cm thick and will fit in the bottom of your margarine tub with about 2cm around the edge, turn it over.

NEIL'S TIP
Plaster of Paris (also known as moulding powder) is available from most major chemists and art shops.

2 Draw your design into the smooth side with a blunt pencil. This can be anything you like – how about your star sign or sun, moon and stars?

3 When you have finished your design, place the plasticine carefully in the bottom of the tub. Press round the edge to fix it down firmly.

4 Mix 3 tablespoons of plaster of Paris with a mug of water. Pour it over your plasticine mould. Dip the middle section of the string into the plaster, then leave this to dry out for a few hours, or overnight.

MIX PLASTER OF PARIS IN AN OLD BOWL OR JUG. NEVER POUR ANY LEFTOVER MIXTURE DOWN THE SINK – PUT IT IN A PLASTIC BAG AND THEN IN A BIN.

5 When it is set, carefully ease your plaster picture out of the mould. Paint it all over in one colour to seal it.

Go over the raised areas in gold or silver pen and tie the string at the back. Now you just have to decide where to hang your brilliant new plaque.

Comic Book Box

Do you leave your comics lying around when you've read them? What you need is a Comic Book Box.

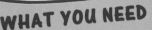
1

Cut the top and side off a cereal box. Draw around the bottom and other side on to a stronger cardboard box. Cut these shapes out and glue them on to the cereal box.

2

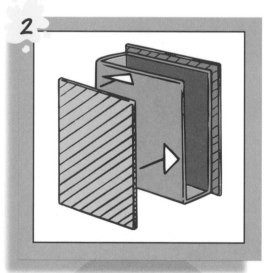

Find a comic that is slightly larger than your cereal box, and draw around this twice on to the cardboard box. Cut out these shapes and glue them on to the front and back of your cereal box.

3

NEIL'S TIP
For added 'comic' effect, bend some of the corners out slightly to make it look like a floppy comic.

Make your box even more solid by covering the outside with a layer of papier mâché (see page 3), going over the edges by about 2cm. Leave this to dry overnight.

When your box is dry, paint it white. Cut out bits from old comics and magazines, and stick them on the front of your box. You can use comic strips, lettering, speech bubbles – anything, even a price. Draw around the items in black pen to give it a professional finish.

I suppose if you ever get tired of your comics, you can always read the box.

Handy Grippers

Can't stick pictures on the wall? Get a grip with this pair of Handy Grippers and put your pictures anywhere you like.

WHAT YOU NEED
thick cardboard, pencil, scissors, paint, felt-tip pens, ruler, glue, picture

1 Place one of your hands on the cardboard so that only your knuckles and fingers are on it. Draw around your closed fingers, gently pushing your pencil between them.

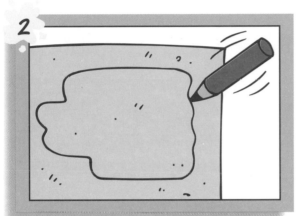

2 Cut it out and draw around it again on another piece of cardboard. Cut this out and you have a pair.

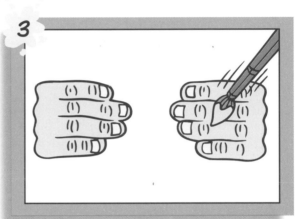

3 Paint them to match your own hands and add detail with felt-tip pens.

4 Draw around a 30cm ruler on to another piece of cardboard and cut it out. From this cut off two individual strips that are the same length as the hands. Then glue these strips on the back of your grippers, at the knuckle end, away from the fingertips.

Gripping stuff!

5 Cut out a piece of card to fit your picture. Place the picture on top, slip on the Handy Grippers and stand your picture wherever you like.

Photo Album House

Have you got photographs of friends or family that you haven't put in an album yet? Why not build them a house – a Photo Album House?

WHAT YOU NEED

two large cereal boxes, scissors, pencil, glue, sticky tape, straws, toothpaste box, toothpaste tube lid, paint, felt-tip pens, photographs

1

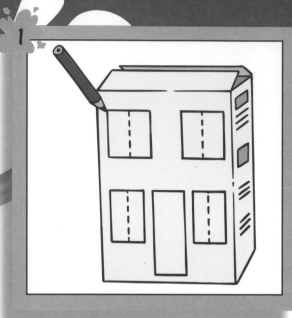

Take one of the cereal boxes. Make sure that the open end is at the top, and draw on the front of your house – four large windows and a door. Leave just enough room for window ledges and lintels (supporting beams across the top of doors and windows), and a nice big doorstep.

2

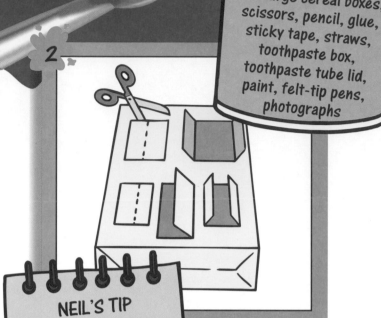

Carefully cut open the door. Then cut the windows to open them up the middle.

NEIL'S TIP

To open up the door and the windows, pop the point of a pencil through each of the corners and carefully cut round three sides of the door, and the top, bottom and centre of the windows.

3

To make the roof, cut the front off the other cereal box and fold it in half. Position it on top of the house, then glue it on to the open top flaps, with a slight overhang.

4

Cut two triangles of card from the second box to fill in the gaps at the side, and tape them securely in place.

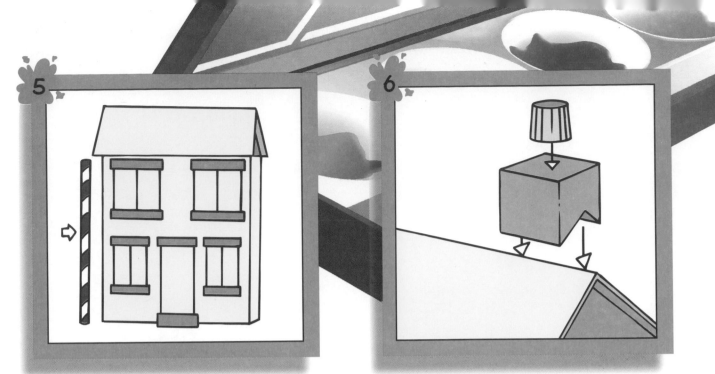

Now add some cardboard strips for window ledges, lintels and the doorstep. Stick on some drinking straws for drainpipes and guttering.

Cut the end off a toothpaste box, snip in two V shapes and place it on the roof. Stick a toothpaste tube lid on top for the chimney.

Then paint your house. It may need a few coats, depending on the colour you choose. When dry, add more detail in felt-tip pen.

Carefully open the bottom of the box. Place some tape on the back of your photos and position them inside your house in line with the windows and door.

Then fold the bottom back together and stand up your Photo Album House.

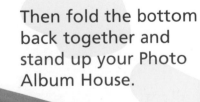

If you've got a lot of photos, you could try building yourself a whole street!

Secret File

Do you have secret notes, photos or letters that you want to hide? You need a Secret File to keep them in.

WHAT YOU NEED
thick cardboard, 2 sheets of A4 paper, pencil, scissors, sticky tape, papier mâché, brown paint, PVA glue, material, ribbon, gold pen, sticky tack

1

Draw around the two sheets of A4 paper on to the cardboard. Cut these out and tape a sheet of paper to each one – on three sides only.

2

Papier mâché both sides, leaving the edge of the pockets open. Push wrinkles into the papier mâché and leave it to dry overnight.

3

Paint both pockets with a layer of brown paint. When dry, cover everything with a layer of PVA glue and let it dry again.

4

CARD
MATERIAL
POCKETS

Lay the pockets side by side about a finger's width apart with the paper face-down and the openings in the middle. Cut a strip of material to cover the join with a small overlap on each side. Stick it in place and leave to dry.

5

NEIL'S TIP
Draw round the edges of the material and the holes with a gold pen to make it look really special.

Using a pencil and a ball of sticky tack, make two holes in each side about 4cm apart just in from the outside edge. Thread some ribbon through to tie the folder closed.

Now you can keep your letters and pictures safe, and hide your secrets in the secret pocket.

Complete Filing System

Are you one of those untidy people who can never find where they have put things? What you need is a Complete Filing System to get you organised.

1

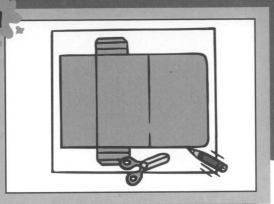

Carefully prise apart the glued edges of the envelope file and lay it out flat. Use this as a template to draw around on to some paper. Cut out as many files as you are going to need.

2

To decorate your files, tear pictures out of old magazines and paste them on to each file. Cover each file front and back, then coat everything in a layer of PVA glue and leave to dry overnight.

3

Fold the files into shape, glue the edges together and leave them to dry.

4

Decide what order you want your files to hang in, then thread the flap of the top file through the coat hanger and tape it on the inside of the crease.

5

Thread some string or ribbon through the gaps at the bottom of the file and tie it in a knot. Then thread the flap of the next file through this string and tape it under the crease again. Carry on like this until all your files are attached.

6

NEIL'S TIP
You can use any kind of paper for this to get different effects— wallpaper, newspaper, scrap paper.

Just fill your files with all your paper, school books and comics and hang them on a hook on your bedroom door, or in your wardrobe, if you want a secret filing system.

Horror Hanger

Are you fed up with people snooping around your wardrobe, taking your clothes or tidying it up? Then scare them off with this Horror Hanger.

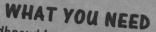
1

Cut out the two big sides of a cardboard box. On one of them draw an ugly, scary face, roughly the same size as your own (not that yours is ugly or scary, of course!). Give it a neck about the length of your pencil. On the other piece, draw around your hands and arms up to your elbows. Cut all of these out and punch a hole with a pencil and a ball of sticky tack in the end of both arms.

2

Twist a piece of magazine paper and tape it in place down one finger and up the arm. Do this for all the fingers, on both sides. You can even add some cardboard cut-out nails.

3

Cover everything front and back with papier mâché – even the nails – just make sure you don't cover the holes that you've made. Then leave them to dry overnight.

4

Model the features of the face with clumps of papier mâché. Cover everything with a layer of flat papier mâché and leave the face to harden overnight.

When the hands and face are dry you can paint them to make them look as horrible as possible. When the paint is dry, tie long pieces of string through the holes in the arms. Tie the other ends to a coat hanger and thread the hands through the sleeves of a shirt or jumper.

Tie a loop of string or wool over the bar in your wardrobe. Tape the head on to the coat hanger and hang it on the string – guaranteed to scare off uninvited guests!

You could do a skeleton design or even a furry werewolf.

No good for me – none of my clothes have sleeves!

Snake Hooks

If your bedroom is so full of junk that you can never find anywhere to put your clothes or bags – you need a Snake Hook.

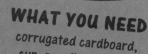

WHAT YOU NEED
corrugated cardboard, cup, pencil, scissors, newspaper, sticky tape, papier mâché, paint, marker pen

1

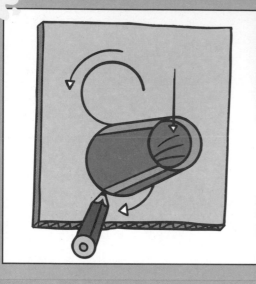

Draw a large 'S' on a piece of corrugated cardboard. An easy way to do this is to draw three quarters of the way around a cup, then move it down and draw three quarters of the way round it again, but the other way.

2

Fatten out your 'S' to make a snake body with a slightly pointy tail and face. Cut it out.

3

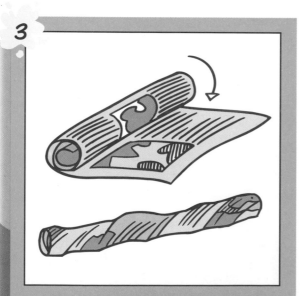

Now take two small sheets of newspaper. Roll each one lengthways, and scrunch it up.

4

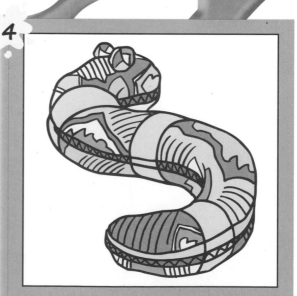

Tape the newspaper to each side of your snake – you may have to tuck in the ends or cut them off. Tape on two small scrunched-up balls of newspaper for eyes.

5

Cover everything with three layers of papier mâché to make your snake hook nice and strong, then leave overnight to dry and harden.

6

Now you can draw a snakey design on it and paint it in bright colours using poster or acrylic paint. When the paint is dry, outline the detail in black marker pen to make it really stand out. Then just hang it up and get hooked.

What sssimply sssensational sssnake hooks! Why not try them in different sizes by drawing round bowls or plates?

23

Art Chart

Art Attack	Date completed
....	....
....	....
....	....
....	....
....	....
....	....
....	....
....	....
....	....
....	....
....	....
....	....
....	....